T0162732

AN EXAMINATION OF THE RELATIONSHIP BETWEEN

CERTIFICATION TEAM EFFECTIVENESS AND TEAM PERFORMANCE

By

Barbara E. Banks-Burton

A Dissertation Submitted in Partial Fulfillment of the

Requirements for the Degree of

Doctor of Philosophy

University of Fairfax

2007

AuthorHouse™
1663 Liberty Drive
Bloomington, IN 47403
www.authorhouse.com
Phone: 1-800-839-8640

©Barbara E. Banks-Burton PhD. All Rights Reserved.

No part of this book may be reproduced, stored in a retrieval system, or transmitted by any means without the written permission of the author.

First published by AuthorHouse 12/29/2009

ISBN: 978-1-4389-7738-6

Library of Congress: 2009914190

Printed in the United States of America
Bloomington, Indiana

This book is printed on acid-free paper.

AN EXAMINATION OF THE RELATIONSHIP BETWEEN

CERTIFICATION TEAM EFFECTIVENESS AND TEAM PERFORMANCE

by

Barbara E. Banks-Burton

has been approved

2007

We hereby certify that this dissertation, submitted by Barbara E. Banks-Burton, conforms to acceptable standards and is fully adequate in scope and quality to fulfill the dissertation requirements for the degree of Doctor of Philosophy.

APPROVED:

Aleksandar Lazarevich, Ph.D.
Chairperson of Dissertation Committee

Lawrence W. Doe, Ph.D.
Dissertation Committee Member

Janice M. Orcutt
Dissertation Committee Member

ACCEPTED AND SIGNED:

Aleksandar Lazarevich, Ph.D.   Date
Chairperson of Dissertation Committee

Victor N. Berlin, Ph.D.   Date
Chief Academic Officer

University of Fairfax

2007

Abstract

An Examination of the Relationship between
Certification Team Effectiveness and Team Performance

by
Barbara E. Banks-Burton

2007

Information technology and E-Government services are vital to the operation of the federal agencies and the functioning of American society as a whole. In the past ten years, and particularly since September 11, 2001, numerous laws, policies, and regulations have been enacted to help secure the federal information infrastructure. Despite legislation and policy changes, and despite annual reports to both the Office of Management and Budget and Congress, the status of the national infrastructure continues to be unsatisfactory.

The literature suggests that modifications to certification and accreditation (C&A) team effectiveness can improve productivity, which in turn, should lead to significant enhancement of information security programs. This study investigated the extent to which team effectiveness affected the cycle time and quality of a key component of the C&A process—the System Security Plan (SSP). The Team Effectiveness Profile (TEP) was utilized to measure the dimensions of team effectiveness among teams assigned to the task of creating an SSP during a three-day training course. Performance of the teams was assessed with respect to cycle time and quality of the SSP produced. The findings indicated that team effectiveness had the potential to influence C&A team performance in the production of the SSP.

Dedication

In loving memory of my father Oscar Banks Jr., my inspiration, and of my dear friends, Michael Mitchell and Andrea Francis, who were my strength. This is also dedicated to my sisters Cynthia and Shona and my Mom who encouraged me via four way phone calls when I was down and needed a boost to stay on track to fulfill my dream.

Acknowledgements

I would like to express my heartfelt appreciation to Dean Janice Orcutt who spent countless hours meeting with me and mentoring me throughout the research process. I am deeply grateful for the role she played as I progressed through my doctoral studies, as she taught me to think as a PhD. Her perseverance, advice and support led me to the completion of this dissertation.

Special thanks to my advisor, Dr. Aleksandar Lazarevich, for his invaluable advice, feedback and encouragement; his vision and motivation helped transform my ideas into substance. A special thank you goes to Dr. Lawrence W. Doe for his support and insight, especially in the early stages of this research. He has been in my corner from the start, willing to help whenever I needed it.

I am also deeply grateful to Dr. Victor Berlin, who has supported me in every way. I thank him for listening patiently to my ideas and encouraging me to pursue them. His willingness to give of his time was a priceless gift. I would also like to thank Janice Berlin for her advice and insight as I developed the topic and wrote this dissertation. She deserves to share the doctorate, given the countless weekends she contributed towards helping me to shape the final product.

I also wish to thank Naomi Weather, Marcus White, Betty and Thresa Lang (NTSI) for reviewing the survey; their suggestions and encouragement were invaluable. In addition, I would like to acknowledge my fellow student, Bettie Ann Graham, who offered encouragement during our study sessions.

I owe a great debt to my family, who helped me through this process; in particular, my sisters who were always there to encourage me when I was tired and wanted to quit. No words can express my appreciation to my parents who always put education first. I thank my daughters, brothers, and sisters for their continuous prayers and support. Special thanks go to my dear friend, who endured the process with me and supported me every step of the way.

Finally, I wish to acknowledge all the members of the intelligence community for their personal sacrifices that enable Americans and others around the world to enjoy the fruits of freedom.

Table of Contents

List of Tables

List of Figures

Chapter 1

Rationale

1.1 Problem Statement

Much of the investment in information security has been ineffective (Farah, 2004). Published Federal Information Security Management Act (FISMA) grades indicate that agencies throughout the government are not meeting expectations with respect to securing the critical information systems infrastructure. These agencies are failing to meet established guidelines, despite federal legislation and policies established by organizations such as the Office of Management and Budget (OMB) and the Central Intelligence Agency (CIA) (Farah, 2004). Thus, Farah (2004) stated that the status of information security programs and practices across the federal agencies remains unacceptable; and further, that although there has been progress in the implementation of security programs (in particular, within the intelligence community) much more remains to be done. Indeed, agency assets and operations that are mission critical are still vulnerable to cyber attacks (Farah, 2004).

Despite spending $4.2 billion in fiscal 2004 on securing information systems, the federal government got a "D+" on its annual security report card (Olsen, 2005). Representing seven percent of the federal government's $59 billion information technology budget in 2004, this grade has caused Congress to increase its scrutiny of the quality and quantity of completed certification and accreditation (C&A) procedures, which are the primary measures of an agency's level of information security (Olsen, 2005).

Furthermore, annually, Congress receives a detailed assessment by the General Accounting Office (GAO), which reports on agency performance of key security practices, as measured by the Inspector General (IG) (OMB, 2002). According to this assessment, the problems that directly influenced certification were: (i) a lack of risk assessments and up-to-date system security plans; (ii) a backlog of properly certified and accredited systems; (iii) inadequate testing and evaluation of systems; and (iv) an absence of backup and contingency planning.

The Memorandum M03-19 (OMB, 2003) stated that in order to achieve an acceptable level of security, 80% of all agency information technology (IT) systems had to be certified and accredited and have security integrated into their lifecycles. This memorandum also suggested that in order to build a successful security program, processes that identify, track, and correct IT security weaknesses had to be incorporated into operations, as supported by the President's FY2004 budget.

Legislation and policy-makers have recognized that the federal information infrastructure must be both secure and reliable (Farah, 2004). With 30 % of agencies being rated as having poor security procedures (Olsen, 2005) and with the expected increase in budgets to $7.3 billion in fiscal year 2010 (INPUT, 2005), federal agencies are feeling the pressure from OMB to have their systems certified and accredited.

Policies such as Director of Central Intelligence Directive 6/3 (DCID 6/3) dictate how systems must be certified and accredited. These policies prescribe the methodology for the C&A process, as well as the documentation requirements for accreditation. These policies state that the System Security Plan (SSP) provides the framework of the C&A process, documents the characteristics and functionality of the system and provides a platform for protecting classified data (CIA, 2000).

Thus, to attain accreditation, the C&A package must consist of the SSP, testing procedures and results, a letter of recommendation, and finally, a letter to authorize the accreditation. The SSP serves as the cornerstone of the certification process because it creates both the baseline of the system and the configuration files to provide what is known in the industry as, the Confidentiality, Integrity, and Availability (CIA) as specified by the National Institute of Standards and Technology (NIST) 800-37 (Ross, Swanson, Stoneburner, Katzke & Johnson, 2004). Without a detailed SSP, agencies have little chance of receiving additional program funding.

Therefore, the efficiency with which the SPP is produced of producing the SSP and the quality of the SSP produced are critical to the effectiveness of a certification and accreditation program (Farah, 2004). As Farah's study suggested, current SSPs are not adequate as measured by FISMA grades, and the status of information security programs across the federal government continues to be unsatisfactory at best.

The process of certification and accreditation was based upon the concept of risk. In any information security program, risk assessment is the critical component ,since it determines the development of security controls for information systems and the associated system security plans required for system certification. Nonetheless, Farah's study revealed that more than 40% of the federal manager respondents (89 out of 214) ranked the certification and accreditation key practice area as a higher priority than the risk assessment key practice area. Clearly, these managers did not recognize the interdependency between the two key practice areas, nor did they understand that risk assessment is the predecessor of certification and accreditation. As Farah noted, these results confirmed that the managers were not sufficiently involved in the C&A process in their agencies.

NIST 800-37 provides a model that describes the certification process as team-oriented. Under NIST 800-37, the process of C&A assesses the level of system security and the level of compliance required by FISMA, both of which are documented in the SSP produced during the process (Ross et al., 2004). This model relies on knowledgeable team members and an effective team environment; otherwise, the performance of the certification team may result in a poor or incomplete SSP, which, in turn, leads to a longer cycle time for producing an appropriate certification package (Olsen, 2005).

> The "Guide for Security Certification and Accreditation of Federal Information Systems" that is published by NIST, defines accreditation as: "The official management decision given by a senior agency official to authorize operation of an information system and to explicitly accept the risk to agency operations, agency assets, or individuals based on the implementation of an agreed-upon set of security controls" (Ross et al., 2004, p. 1).

The systems of the nation's critical infrastructure are the foundation of national security; and if not properly certified and accredited, these systems are vulnerable to an increased risk of attack and penetration (Farah, 2004). Agencies rely on the C&A process as the primary vehicle for risk management (OMB, 2002). This has created a heavy demand on certification teams to certify and accredit information systems. Furthermore, a backlog of information systems requiring certification and accreditation has accumulated because of the poor quality of the SSP's being produced and the long cycle time to produce them (Olsen, 2005).

As the output of a team's task, time and quality are measures of team performance. A review of the literature indicated that team effectiveness affects team performance. Team effectiveness is the measure of how well a team interacts to achieve its goal, and is therefore, an internal measure of the team itself.

Furthermore, according to Glaser (1989), Ting (1991), and Wetherbe (1995), team effectiveness was a primary factor in driving team performance and reducing cycle time. Glaser also identified five dimensions of team effectiveness:

1. mission and goals

2. organization (roles)

3. operating processes

4. intra-group relationships

5. inter-team relations

Finally, research by Grütter, Field, and Faull (2002) posited that high-performing teams work more productively and therefore shorten cycle times, which, in turn, can lead to cost reduction.

1.2 Contribution to Knowledge

Currently, the expenditures for information security programs are not yielding the level of compliance expected (Olsen, 2005). Based upon a review of the literature, the researcher believed that understanding the relationship between team effectiveness and team performance could provide organizations with greater insight on constructing effective teams to perform the certification and accreditation of the critical security system infrastructure to improve FISMA compliance. In addition, the researcher believed that examining C&A team performance could lead to operational benefits such as reducing

C&A backlogs, improving tracking of systems, securing assets, and reducing the cost of

information security programs.

While Farah's study (2004) explored the relationship between the status of FISMA

compliance and the quality of C&A processes, currently no published research in the

information assurance domain has examined the relationship between certification team

effectiveness and the quality of the SSP produced by the team. Therefore, this exploratory

study extends the research on information security compliance by examining the

relationship between team effectiveness and team performance, measured by both the

quality of the SSP and the cycle time required to produce it.

1.3 Research Questions

Specifically, the researcher investigated whether team effectiveness had a

significant influence on the cycle time it took to produce the SSP and the quality of the SSP

produced.

Thus, the research questions that guided this study were as follows:

1. Is there a relationship between certification team effectiveness and team
   performance?

2. Is there a relationship between any specific dimension of team effectiveness and
   team performance?

Chapter 2

Literature Review

This review of literature investigated the primary components of this study: teams and team effectiveness, the measurement of team performance, factors affecting team performance, and the influence of team effectiveness on team performance.

2.1 Teams and Work Groups

Teams are differentiated from work groups in research literature. Although "team" and "work group" are often used interchangeably, the difference is that a team has shared or common goals, whereas a work group may not (Mason, 1999). The study of teams in the work environment has been researched for several decades (Drucker, 1973; Dyer, 1987; Francis & Young, 1979; Glaser, 1989; Yoon, 2005; Zaccaro, Rittman, & Marks, 2001). This research defined the following characteristics of a team:

- Team members have distinct roles.

- Teams have goals that unite them.

- Teams have open communication among their members.

- Teams are empowered to act.

These characteristics have led to a widely accepted definition of a team as expressed in 1989 by Nolan: "a group of people working together to achieve common objectives and who are willing to forego individual autonomy to the extent necessary to achieve those objectives" (p. 227).

The absence of teamwork, at any level, can limit organizational effectiveness and eventually kill an organization (Maddux, 1989). As the role of teams in organizations has grown in importance, research has been driven by the need to understand both how to measure and how to increase team effectiveness (Nolan, 1989).

2.2 Teams and Team Effectiveness

Table 1 identifies the primary studies reviewed for the purposes of understanding which characteristics are significant in identifying an effective team. This body of research suggested that several characteristics form the fundamental baseline of an effective team (Buchholz & Roth, 1987; Glaser, 1989; Nolan, 1989). However, individual studies had varying interpretations of the relative importance of these characteristics. The four most commonly studied characteristics of effective teams in the literature were:

1. common purpose, mission, and goals

2. roles and shared responsibility

3. task orientation and operating processes

4. communication and relations within and among groups.

Table 1

Characteristics of Effective Teams

Source	Participative Leadership	Common Purpose, Mission, Goals	Roles, Shared Responsibility	Focus on Tasks, Operating Processes	Communication, Trust, Interpersonal Relations	Talent Creation	Future Focus	Rapid Response
Anderson & Franks, 2001	X	X	X	X	X	X		X
Blackburn, Scudder, & Van Wassenhove, 1996	X	X	X		X			X
Buchholz & Roth, 1987	X	X	X		X	X	X	X
Cranton & Webber, 2005		X	X	X				
Dyer, 1987		X	X		X			
Edwards & Sridhar, 2003			X		X			
Farah, 2004		X	X	X				X
Fernandez, 2003		X	X	X	X			
Ferraiolo, Williams, & Landoll, 1994		X	X	X	X			X
Glaser & Glaser, 1989		X	X	X				X
Grütter, Field, & Faull, 2002	X	X	X	X	X			X
Harrison, Mohammed, McGrath, Florey & Vanderstoep, 2003		X	X	X	X			X
Holton, 2001		X	X	X	X			X
Hult, Frolick, & Nichols, 1995		X	X	X	X			X
Janz, 1996		X	X	X				X
Offerman & Spiros, in press		X	X	X	X			X
Olsen, 2005				X	X			
Ramadorai & Harris, 2003	X		X					
Rangarajan, Chonko, Jones, & Roberts, 2004		X	X	X				
Ross, Swanson, Stoneburner, Katzke, & Johnson, 2004		X	X	X				
Sashkin & Burke, 1987		X	X	X				X
Syamil, Doll & Apigian, 2004		X	X	X	X			
Ting, 1991		X	X	X	X			X
Trent, 2004		X		X	X			
Varney, 1989		X	X	X	X			
Werner & Lester, 2001		X	X		X			
Zaccaro, Rittman, & Marks, 2001			X		X			X

9

Buchholz and Roth (1987), described an effective team as a synergistic team. They posited that an effective team is a high performance team, where the total effect of the team effort is greater than the sum of all indiviual efforts of the team members. Further; they identified eight characteristics of effective teams as follows:

- Participative leadership: The leader of the team creates an environment of interdependency and encourages team decision-making and consensus.

- Common purpose: The team shares a common goal that requires the talents and abilities of all team members.

- Focus on task: The energy of the team members is focused on the purpose or task, whether they are together or alone.

- Shared responsibility: Team members are accountable for their individual contribution to the collective results.

- High level of communication: An environment where team members can experience trust and support is actively fostered.

- Talent creation: The team consists of indiviuals who can apply their talents and creativity to the team objectives, while developing new skills and insights from each other.

- Future-focused: A positive attitude toward change exists and team members anticipate future needs and identify opportunties for innovation.

- Rapid response: The team reacts rapidly to new priorities and needs, developing action plans that support success.

These characteristics have been commonly accepted in on team effectiveness. Of these characteristics, the importance of clearly defined roles and team structure, were identified as the most critical elements (Buchholz & Roth, 1987). For example, Fernandez (2003) conducted a study of the effectiveness of small student groups working together for school assignments. His study had implications in three areas related to team effectiveness as identified by Glaser and Glaser (1989). The study showed that: (a) working in teams allowed individuals to differentiate their roles based on their expertise; (b) good interpersonal relationships had a positive impact on group performance; and (c) shared goals resulted in greater confidence and increased team performance.

Anderson and Frank's (2001) study showed that a division of labor and coordinated concurrent action is necessary in order to have an effective team. Anderson, Franks, and McShea (2001) viewed that a "team" carries out a "team task" meaning, "it *necessarily* requires *different individuals* to perform *different subtasks concurrently*" (p. 291).

Holton (2001) concluded that every member of an effective team has a preferred role or set of roles. He found that ambiguity in the roles of the team members led to an imbalance in the team, which reduced its effectiveness. Holton's study further suggested that teams in which roles were clearly defined and understood achieved better performance. Furthermore, the results achieved by such teams were more effective than those achieved by any one individual.

In studying the performance of teams, Varney (1989) identified the following factors as necessary for the success of a team:

- Roles are clear to each person.

- Individuals are committed to their jobs, and accept and support the roles of others.

- Team goals are as important as individual goals.

- Practices, structure, and policies are understood and agreed to by all team members.

- Open and helpful relations and communication are essential.

From this review of the literature, the researcher identified several models used in previous studies of team effectiveness. However, it is the Team Effectiveness Profile (TEP), developed by Glaser and Glaser (1989), which most closely aligned with Varney's findings.

This model utilized five dimensions to measure the effectiveness of a team:

1. Mission and goals

2. Organization (roles)

3. Operating processes

4. Intra-group relationships

5. Inter-team relations

Of particular interest to the researcher was the dissertation research conducted by Ting (1991), which studied the relationship between team effectiveness and team performance in a high-technology environment utilizing the TEP instrument to measure team effectiveness. Moreover, the specific use of cycle time and quality to measure team performance was particularly relevant to this dissertation study.

2.3 Factors Affecting Team Performance

A review of the literature revealed several factors that affect the performance of work teams (Anderson & Franks, 2001; Mason, 1999). Table 2 identifies the most common of these factors and summarizes the findings of research reviewed which related to the influence of each factor on team performance. It should be noted that, in many cases, these factors were not studied individually as the only variable affecting performance. Rather, they were most often studied as intervening variables that influenced performance.

Increasingly, an important focus of management is the measurement of productivity and the quality of work performed by the team (Nolan, 1989). NIST 800-37 states that team characteristics can affect the quality of the C&A team deliverables, which are in part a result of the C&A process (Ross et al., 2004).

A measurement of performance in any process includes cycle time and level of quality. While complexity and procedural factors have the potential to affect organizational performance, reduced cycle times are widely considered measures of the level of process improvements achieved by a team (Hult, Ketchen, & Nichols, 2002). As indicated by Ross et al. (2004), it is critical for government agencies to develop an appropriate strategy for addressing the highly variable costs of implementing complex security systems. Managing cycle time is a significant aspect of such a strategy.

Table 2

Factors Influencing Team Performance

Factor	Description of Findings	Sources Reviewed
Team Composition	Attributes such as group size and demographic characteristics (such as age and gender) have been found to have significant influence on the performance of a team.	• Anderson & Franks, 2001 • Blackburn, Scudder, & Van Wassenhove, 1996 • Chowdhury, 2005 • Cramton & Webber, 2005 • Janz, 1996 • Trent, 2004 • Werner & Lester, 2001
Team Cohesion	The degree to which team members are willing to stay together (whether voluntary or under pressure) has been found to have an effect on performance.	• Anderson & Franks, 2001 • Anderson, Franks & McShea, 2001 • Harrison, Mohammed, McGrath, Florey, & Vanderstoep, 2003 • Janz, Prakash, & Frolick, 1997 • Trent, 2004 • Werner & Lester, 2001
Team Norms	Shared expectations of behavior related to efficiency and quality control have been shown to have a positive influence on team performance.	• Anderson & Franks, 2001 • Anderson, Franks & McShea, 2001 • Harrison, Mohammed, McGrath, Florey, & Vanderstoep, 2003 • Ramadorai, A. & Harris, J. 2003 • Zaccaro, Rittman & Marks, 2001
Team Roles	Clear definition of roles and responsibilities and their acceptance by team members have been shown to greatly influence performance of a team.	• Anderson & Franks, 2001 • Anderson, Franks & McShea, 2001 • Blackburn, Scudder, & Van Wassenhove, 1996 • Edwards & Sridhar, 2003 • Janz, 1996 • Ramadorai, A. & Harris, J. (2003 • Werner & Lester, 2001
Leadership	Research has indicated that the expectations of a leader can influence (both positively and negatively) the performance of a team.	• Anderson & Franks, 2001 • Blackburn, Scudder, & Van Wassenhove, 1996 • Day, Gronn & Salas, 2004 • Janz, Prakash, & Frolick, 1997 • Ramadorai, A. & Harris, J. (2003 • Yoon, 2005 • Zaccaro, Rittman & Marks, 2001

Table 2: (cont.)
Factors Influencing Team Performance

Factor	Description of Findings	Sources Reviewed
Team Goals	The acceptance of the priority of the group goals over individual goals has been shown to have an influence on the performance of a team.	• Grütter, Field & Faull, 2002 • Linderman, Schroeder & Choo, in press • Syamil, Doll & Apigian, 2004 • Trent, 2004 • Werner & Lester, 2001
Consequences	Rewards or incentives that are contingent on performance have repeatedly been shown to have a positive influence on team performance.	• Grütter, Field & Faull, 2002 • Rangarajan, D., Chonko, L.B., Jones, E., & Roberts, J.A. (2004 • Syamil, Doll & Apigian, 2004 • Trent, 2004 • Yoon, 2005
Interdependency	When performance relies on interdependency of behaviors among members, individuals become responsible to each other. The acceptance of this responsibility influences team performance.	• Anderson, Franks & McShea, 2001 • Grütter, Field & Faull, 2002 • Harrison, Mohammed, McGrath, Florey, & Vanderstoep, 2003 • Kim & Burns, 2001 • Rangarajan, Chonko, Jones, & Roberts, J.A. 2004
Empowerment	The degree to which a team is able to self-manage and self-regulate group behavior on highly related tasks has been found to have a significant influence on team performance.	• Bengtsson, 1999 • Day, Gronn & Salas, 2004 • Janz, 1996 • Janz, Prakash, & Frolick, 1997 • Yoon, 2005 • Zaccaro, Rittman & Marks, 2001
Communication	Coordination of events, open communication among members, trust, and feedback have been shown to affect team performance.	• Edwards & Sridhar, 2003 • Grütter, Field & Faull, 2002 • Janz, 1996 • Trent, 2004 • Yoon, 2005 • Zaccaro, Rittman & Marks, 2001
Mission and Vision	Clear understanding of team mission and vision have been found to influence the performance of a team.	• Buchholz & Roth, 1987 • Fernandez, 2003 • Glaser & Glaser, 1989 • Varney, 1989

The concept of cycle time has been studied with respect to productivity in processes that mirror the C&A process. For example, Blackburn, Scudder, and Van Wassenhove (1996) suggested that time is an essential measure of performance in the product development process. In that study of the effect of management practices on software development processes, the authors found that higher productivity was achieved when development processes were accelerated. They concluded that time delays can affect projects in a number of ways, with cost overruns being the primary result. Separate studies by Wetherbe (1995) and Janz (1996) suggested that reducing cycle time played a significant role in minimizing cost overruns.

Process performance in product development is a measure of how effectively the development team worked together (Syamil, Doll, & Apigian, 2004). In evaluating process performance, Syamil et al. (2004) evaluated teamwork and its relationship to team productivity and cycle time for engineering changes. They observed that the characteristics of effective teams included successful communication, effectual conflict resolution skills, and good coordination of tasks and roles. The authors stated further that team effectiveness was essential because it reduced project time, which in turn, reduced cost and ultimately improved the quality of the product.

2.4 Team Effectiveness and Team Performance

As mentioned previously, research has suggested that an effective team can produce better results than can individual performance. In fact, the team has been recognized as the building block of an organization (Holton, 2001). Research has posited that an effective team depends upon characteristics such as competence, team make-up, team efficiency, and team organization (Glaser, 1989; Anderson & Franks, 2001; Anderson, Franks & McShea, 2001). In addition, they stated that team effectiveness was dynamically interrelated with organizational context, boundaries, and team development. Team effectiveness was defined by Edmonston, Roberto & Watkins (2003) as the degree to which a team makes decisions and implements processes that enhance team performance.

In a study of student performance, Werner and Lester (2001) utilized a framework for team effectiveness that incorporated team structure, team spirit, social support, workload sharing, and intra-group communication. In that study, the authors used team satisfaction and team grades as measures of team performance. Their findings confirmed a significant correlation between team structure and performance, and further suggested important relationships between goal clarity and team performance and commitment and team performance.

Ramadorai and Harris (2003) conducted a study comparing the engineering effectiveness of several market leaders and found some best-in-class tendencies. Their findings suggested that cycle time, effort, predictability, and quality were factors that influenced best-in-class performance. The findings also suggested that the companies exhibiting these characteristics were able to offer their customers integrated solutions that addressed their needs, as opposed to just an accumulation of products.

In studying the performance of teams, Varney (1989) identified specific characteristics as necessary for the success of the team. These characteristics were as follows:

- Roles are clear to each person

- Individuals are committed to their jobs, and accept and support the roles of others

- Team goals are as important as individual goals

- Practices, structure, and policies are understood and agreed to by all team members

- Open and helpful relations and communication are essential.

Research further suggested that these characteristics form the fundamental baseline of an effective team (Buchholz & Roth, 1987; Glaser, 1989; Nolan, 1989).

2.5 Opportunity for Contribution

In the last ten years, a significant amount of research has been performed in the area of team effectiveness. Table 1 identifies several characteristics of an effective team and lists many researchers that have conducted studies in this area. However, an opportunity exists to investigate the relationship between team effectiveness and team performance in the context of security -- specifically in the study of C&A teams and their performance. In utilizing one of the team effectiveness models, TEP, the researcher believed that it was possible to gain insight into which dimensions of team effectiveness (mission/goals, roles/organization, process, and communication) have the greatest impact on the efficient production of quality team deliverables.

Chapter 3

Theoretical Framework

In this study, the researcher applied theory and findings from team effectiveness and team performance research literature to the C&A process, and extended Glaser's (1989) research, by using Ting's (1991) dissertation research (in a high-technology environment) as a model. Ting's research was influenced by Dyer's (1987) theory that team effectiveness is essential in organizational development and Glaser's (1989) theory that team effectiveness greatly influences job performance. Furthermore, as was discussed in Chapter 2, Ting's research examined the relationship between team effectiveness and team performance, using two specific characteristics of team performance – cycle time and quality. In so doing, Ting utilized the Team Effectiveness Profile (TEP) instrument developed by Glaser and Glaser in 1989 to measure team effectiveness. This instrument measured five dimensions of team effectiveness:

- mission and goals,

- team roles,

- operating processes,

- intra-group relationships, and

- inter-team relations.

Research has suggested that team effectiveness is a fundamental element in improving quality and productivity in an organization, as a whole, particularly when evaluating processes (Ferraiolo, Williams, & Landoll, 1994). The sequence of process improvement begins with knowledge and knowledge influences team characteristics (Almond & Verba, 1963). Almond and Verba (1963) believed that positive team characteristics stimulate the achievement of knowledge and skills needed for successful implementation. On the other hand, the absence of positive team characteristics, at any level, can limit organizational effectiveness, can provoke resistance to new initiatives, and can create roadblocks to implementation (Varney, 1989). The cognitive and effectiveness characteristics of teams are interrelated, each influencing the other, and both affecting higher performance.

Using this process framework as a basis, the researcher developed Figure 1 to illustrate the relationship between team effectiveness and knowledge, and their combined influence on organizational performance.

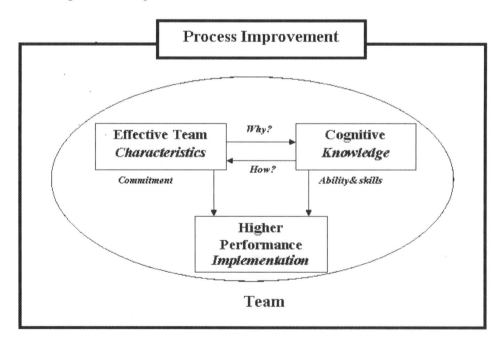

Figure 1. Effective-Cognitive-Higher Performance Model

3.1 Defining the Dependent Variable

As mentioned previously, the System Security Plan (SSP) is a required deliverable of the C&A process. Thus, the dependent variable of this study was team performance, as defined by two characteristics of the SSP production: cycle time and product quality. As discussed in Chapter 1, the efficiency of producing the SSP and the quality of the SSP produced are critical to the effectiveness of a C&A program.

With respect to task or process outcome, quality improvements have been considered a measure of team performance. Studies have linked improved quality with cost reductions (Janz, 1996), which is an important outcome in light of the current budgets of federal agencies. Janz (1996) also noted that, although the goal of cycle time reduction is to reduce processing time, cycle time reduction also results in improved product quality. Janz, Prakash, and Frolick (1997) stated that best practice studies confirmed that when system development cycle time was approached from a technological perspective, incremental improvements occurred; however, greater improvements in the speed and quality of the system development process more often resulted when workforce or team-based solutions were applied.

3.1.1 Cycle Time

Cycle time is the total time from the beginning to the end of a defined process, such as the creation of the System Security Plan (SSP). Cycle time includes process time, which is time spent taking action to progress toward completion, and delay time, which is time spent waiting for the next action to take place. In other words, cycle time is the total elapsed time to move a unit of work from the beginning to the end of a physical process (Blackburn, Scudder, & Van Wassenhove, 1996).

3.1.2 Quality of Product

Webster (2003) defined quality as "a degree or grade of excellence". Quality itself is fundamentally relational: "Quality is the ongoing process of building and sustaining relationships by assessing, anticipating, and fulfilling stated and implied needs" (Winder & Judd, 1996, n.p.).

The quality of the System Security Plan in this study was defined as the completeness of the SSP with respect to the specified security requirements.

3.2 Defining the Independent Variable

The independent variable in this study was team effectiveness. As was discussed in Chapter 2, the Ting dissertation (1991) served as a model for this study, given its specific use of cycle time and product quality as dependent variables. Ting's study demonstrated that team effectiveness could be measured using Glaser's TEP instrument. In addition, the researcher determined that the Team Effectiveness Profile (TEP) captured the characteristics most applicable to the certification team environment.

In this study, team effectiveness was evaluated according to the five dimensions of the TEP which were defined as follows:

1. Mission, planning and goal setting: Team members understand the mission and objectives of the project and develop a plan for completion.

2. Organization: The role of each team member is clearly identified; each member is responsible for his/her contribution and accountable for completion.

3. Operating processes: Procedures are implemented to successfully accomplish the objectives, with specific concern for problem-solving, decision-making, conflict management, and meeting quality standards.

4. Intra-group relationships: Open and honest communication is encouraged and supported within the group.

5. Inter-team relations: Working relationships exist that facilitate the sharing of knowledge among groups.

3.3 Hypotheses

As stated in Chapter 1, this study was guided by the following research questions:

1. Is there a relationship between certification team effectiveness and team performance?

2. Is there a relationship between any specific dimension of team effectiveness and team performance?

To explore these questions, the researcher posed the following hypotheses:

- H1: There will be a positive correlation between team effectiveness and the cycle time required to complete the System Security Plan (SSP).

- H2: There will be a positive correlation between team effectiveness and the quality of the SSP produced by the team.

- H3: There will be a positive correlation between an individual dimension of team effectiveness and the cycle time required to complete the System Security Plan (SSP).

- H4: There will be a positive correlation between an individual dimension of team effectiveness and the quality of the SSP produced by the team.

3.4 Alternative Explanations

Research suggests that factors other than team effectiveness can explain team performance when evaluating cycle time and quality. In the research reviewed in Chapter 2, five variables appeared to have the most significant influence on team performance as described below:

1. Complexity of information system: Systems range from stand-alone to enterprise-wide infrastructures with access ranging from single users to multi-complex nodes (Blackburn, Scudder, & Van Wassenhove, 1996).

2. Time scheduling: Geographically dispersed work groups, availability, and conflicting work priorities impose time constraints (Cramton & Webber, 2005;

Edwards & Sridhar, 2003; Harrison, Mohammed, McGrath, Florey, & Vanderstoep, 2003).

3. Technical competencies: Teams are composed of individuals with varying levels of competency and system familiarity (Blackburn, Scudder, & Van Wassenhove, 1996).

4. Consequences: Compensation rewards such as promotions or pay can drive performance (Offermann, & Spiros, in press; Rangarajan, Chonko, Jones, & Roberts, 2004).

5. Familiarity with the methodology: Team members have varying levels of understanding and experience with C&A processes (Harrison et al., 2003; Sashkin & Burke, 1987).

3.5 Implications for Design

Within normal work environments, each of the aforementioned variables can affect C&A team members and their performance. Therefore, for the purposes of this study, a classroom environment was used as the test setting. Given this environment, the design of this study controlled for these factors as follows:

1. Complexity of information system: Using a case study that outlined a simplified IS environment; the research participants all evaluated the same information system for which they produced an SSP document.

2. Time scheduling: Research participants were allotted equal time to produce an SSP as a scheduled class project.

3. Technical competency: The case study did not require specific technical knowledge, experience, or certifications and was presented at a level easily understood by entry-level certifiers.

4. Consequences: There were no incentives such as extra pay, bonuses or promotions offered with respect to participation in this course. Similarly, no negative consequences existed with respect to not performing well within the course.

5. Familiarity with the methodology: The course provided training on a specific approach to creating the required course deliverable, the SSP.

Chapter 4

Research Methodology

4.1 Project History

The researcher has been employed in the IA arena for the past 12 years and has observed successes and failures of C&A teams over the course of those years. The researcher observed that differences in team relationships appeared to affect the performance of the teams when completing C&A tasks. This led to an investigation into the factors that could improve team performance, particularly with respect to the role of team effectiveness in the timely delivery of quality results.

The opportunity to study team dynamics in a controlled environment presented itself in the form of a training course designed to teach certification processes to new certifiers. Using the guidelines and policies set forth by the intelligence community (DCID 6/3) for classified systems processing sensitive compartmented information (SCI) data, the participants of this course were trained to develop an SSP (the final deliverable of the C&A process). At the end of the training period, the participants were grouped into teams of two to three to produce this document.

In the initial stages of this study, the researcher evaluated various models that were used to measure team effectiveness and determined that the Team Effectiveness Profile

(TEP) developed by Glaser and Glaser (1989) was the most appropriate instrument for use in this study. This instrument measured five dimensions of team effectiveness that reflected the characteristics of a certification team, as outlined in NIST guidelines (2004).

A pilot test of the TEP instrument was conducted during a single course in December 2005. It was determined that the instrument adequately measured the dimensions of team effectiveness of greatest interest to the researcher; however, the participants suggested that there was confusion as to whether the questions applied to the teams to which they were assigned within the course or the teams with whom they normally worked at their place of employment. As a result, the researcher modified the original TEP questions to reflect the team experience within the training course, rather than the team experience in the workplace.

Data were then collected during two course sessions conducted in April 2006.

4.2 Context of Study

4.2.1 Setting

This study was conducted during a training course that simulated the processes that lead to the development of the SSP. The three-day course was conducted at the National Security Training Institute (NSTI) in Chantilly, Virginia. Typically, 25 to 30 professionals seeking training on the certification requirements of DCID 6/3 are enrolled in the course.

The training activities provided the participants with an understanding of how to prepare the documentation of an automated information system's security posture. Additionally, participants learned how to rate the protection level (PL) and level of concern

(LOC), two primary measures used in assessing the performance of a system (see Appendix C).

On the third day of training, teams of two or three individuals were formed by the instructor. The instructor attempted to balance the team composition with respect to technical background and years of experience. To measure whether the participants learned the security requirements and safeguards of certifying a system, the instructor assigned a group project, which required each team to evaluate a simple automated information system and to produce an SSP, which documented the system's security posture. To complete this project, each team was provided the identical scenario and supporting material, and was asked to develop an SSP, given the security requirements specified. Teams were given a maximum of four hours to complete the SSP document.

4.2.2 Population Studied

Participants in the course included professionals such as certifiers, system administrators, end-users, and other security-related personnel from the intelligence community. These professionals were all U.S. citizens, with a variety of educational levels, work experience, and ages. Participants attended this course to gain the knowledge and skills required to perform C&A. Most participants were enrolled by their employers either because they had been recently assigned to a C&A team, or had such an assignment pending.

Two course sessions labeled Group A and Group B were included in this study. The details are shown in Table 3.

Table 3
Population Information

Section	Location	Date	Number of Students	Number of Teams
Group A	Dulles VA	April 18, 2006	19	8
Group B	Washington DC	April 25, 2006	15*	5

Note. One team from Group B was eliminated from the sample because they left prior to the completion of the course decreasing the number of participants from 17 to 15.

The following section presents the demographic data collected.

Gender:

Table 4 summarizes the gender distribution of Groups A and B, as well as the sample total. Participants in this study were predominantly male (64.7%).

Table 4
Gender Distribution

	Group A		Group B		Total	
Gender	Count	Percentage	Count	Percentage	Count	Percentage
Male	13	68.4	9	60.0	22	64.7
Female	6	31.6	6	40.0	12	35.3
Total	19	100.0	15	100.0	34	100.0

Age:

Table 5 summarizes the age distribution of Groups A and B. Participants in this study represented most age groups, with the largest number (13) in the age range of 46-54 (38.2%), followed by those in the age range of 36-45 (26.5%)

Table 5
Age Distribution

	Group A		Group B		Total	
Age Range	Count	Percentage	Count	Percentage	Count	Percentage
Under 25	0	0.00	0	0.00	0	0.0
26 – 35	3	15.79	3	20.00	6	17.6
36 – 45	7	36.84	2	13.33	9	26.5
46 – 54	5	26.32	8	53.33	13	38.2
55 +	4	21.05	2	13.33	6	17.6
Total	19	100.00	15	100.00	34	100.0

Education Level:

Table 6 summarizes the distribution of participants with respect to education levels.

Fifty percent (50%) of the sample held Baccalaureate (BA/BS) degrees, while the

remaining participants held either Master's degrees (26.5%) or High School diplomas

(20.6%). Only one participant indicated an educational level outside of these categories and

none of the participants held a doctorate.

Table 6
Education Level Distribution

	Group A		Group B		Total	
Education	Count	Percentage	Count	Percentage	Count	Percentage
HS or GED	2	10.5	5	33.3	7	20.6
B.A. or B.S.	11	57.9	6	40.0	17	50.0
M.A. or M.S.	5	26.3	4	26.7	9	26.5
Ph.D.	0	0.0	0	0.0	0	0.0
Other	1	05.3	0	0.0	1	2.9
Total	19	100.0	15	100.0	34	100.0

Work Experience with SSP:

Table 7 summarizes the distribution of participants with respect to the number of years of experience they possessed working with SSP development. The majority of the participants (64.7%) reported having experience of one year or less.

Table 7
Work Experience with SSP

Experience	Group A		Group B		Total	
	Count	Percentage	Count	Percentage	Count	Percentage
None	5	26.3	5	33.3	10	29.4
< 1 year	5	26.3	5	33.3	10	29.4
1 year	2	10.5	0	0	2	5.9
2 years	0	0.0	2	13.3	2	5.9
3 years	4	21.1	2	13.3	6	17.6
5 years >	3	15.8	1	06.7	4	11.8
Total	19	100.0	15	100.0	34	100.0

Professions:

Table 8 summarizes the distribution of participants with respect to profession. The largest percentage of participants (41.2%) identified themselves as Information Security professionals.

Table 8
Professions

Professions	Group A		Group B		Total	
	Count	Percentage	Count	Percentage	Count	Percentage
Auditing	0	0.0	1	6.7	1	2.9
Information Security	7	36.8	7	46.7	14	41.2
Information Technology	6	31.6	1	6.7	7	20.6
Other	6	31.6	6	40.0	12	35.3
Total	19	100.0	15	100.0	34	100.0

Security Environment:

Table 9 summarizes the distribution of participants with respect to the security environment in which they worked. More than 85% of the participants worked in a combined classified and unclassified environment, with the remaining participants identifying their work environment as classified-only. None of the participants reported that they worked in an unclassified-only environment.

Table 9
Security Work Environment

Security Environment	Group A		Group B		Total	
	Count	Percentage	Count	Percentage	Count	Percentage
Classified only	3	15.8	2	13.3	5	14.7
Classified/ Unclassified	16	84.2	13	86.7	29	85.3
Unclassified only	0	0.0	0	0.0	0	0.0
Total	19	100.0	15	100.0	34	100.0

4.2.3 Limitations

This research was an exploratory extension of Glaser's (1989) previous work as applied to information security, using Ting's research (1991) as a model. This study does not make claims of generalizability, due to the convenience sampling utilized in this design. These course-based team assignments do not reflect the size of a team normally assigned to the C&A process within the work place. In addition, the sample studied may not be representative of the skills and experience typically found in C&A teams within the workplace.

Another possible limitation of the study was that participants were not asked whether English was their first language. It is possible that if language issues were present, some of the questions in the TEP and demographic survey, as well as the instructions given for the assignments, could have been misinterpreted.

4.3 Data Collected

To measure the independent variable, team effectiveness, the study employed Glaser's Team Effectiveness Profile (TEP), an accepted instrument that measures team effectiveness using five key dimensions: mission, vision, and goals; team roles; operating procedures; interpersonal relationships among team members; and inter-team relationships. The modified TEP surveys were distributed to course participants in order to collect data on their perception of the effectiveness of the team to which they were assigned for producing the SSP. The TEP provided a means of calculating a total effectiveness score for each team based on the perceptions of team members.

The first measure of the dependent variable, the cycle time required by each team to produce the SSP, was the self-reported completion time for the course project.

The second measure of the dependent variable, the quality of the SSP produced, was the level of completeness and appropriateness of the security settings and test verifications included in the SSP produced by the team. Using a checklist of required items to be included in the SSP, the instructor assigned a numerical score for the SSP, based on the presence (or absence) of these items for both Groups A and B.

4.4 Instrumentation

To collect the data for measuring team effectiveness and demographic variables, the study employed two instruments:

4.4.1 Team Effectiveness Profile

The Team Effectiveness Profile (TEP) was utilized to measure team effectiveness (see Appendix D). Organization Design and Development, Inc. published this questionnaire in 1980; it consists of 50 Likert-type items that measure team effectiveness, using the five dimensions previously described in this study. The TEP is a tested instrument, which has been used for studies of groups of varying sizes. In 1980 and 1984, the University Research Group in Philadelphia validated the questionnaire. In 1980, to prove the validity of the questionnaire, split-half reliability checks on groups were conducted to measure consistency in responses within the groups (Glaser, 1989). As was discussed earlier, the Ting study (1991), upon which this research was modeled, utilized the TEP to measure team effectiveness.

The 50 questions addressed Glaser's five dimensions of team effectiveness utilizing the following distribution:

Mission	10 items
Organization	10 items
Operating Processes	10 items
Intragroup Relations	10 items
Inter-team Relations	10 items

Research participants were asked to rate each item using a five-point scale, which ranged from one (never) to five (always).

5	Team <u>always</u> did this
4	Team <u>usually</u> did this
3	Team <u>sometimes</u> did this
2	Team <u>usually did not</u> do this
1	Team <u>never</u> did this

Based on the ratings of each team member, a team score was determined for each of the five dimensions, as well as a total Team Effectiveness Score. Using this Team Effectiveness Score, the level of effectiveness of the team was classified as follows:

<u>Range</u>	<u>Description of Team Effectiveness</u>
50-133	Immature: Dependent on leader
134-160	Fragmented: Conflicts present
161-188	Cohesive: Strong interpersonal relationships and allegiances
189-215	Effective: Work well as a group on tasks and process
216-250	Synergistic: Highly developed and interdependent

The individual dimension scores helped to determine the level of effectiveness exhibited for each dimension (goals/missions; roles; operating processes; interpersonal relationships; and inter-team relationships) and, as such, identified which dimensions needed improvement.

4.4.2 Demographic Questionnaire

The researcher developed the demographic questionnaire using the instrument found in the Farah (2004) dissertation as a model. The demographic survey consisted of ten questions. Eight of these questions concerned the following areas:

- Gender

- Age

- Education

- Security Certifications

- Classification of work environment

- Experience in Security

The two remaining questions were designed to test each participant's knowledge and skills in assessing the Protection Level (PL) and Level of Concern (LOC) that are associated with an information system (see Appendix E).

4.5 Methodology

The Team Effectiveness Profile and demographic questionnaires were administered at the conclusion of a three-day training program, in which the participants learned the procedures and requirements specified by DCID 6/3 in developing the SSP.

This research used a mixed-method approach to analyze the variables identified for study: team effectiveness and team performance. Convenience sampling of training course participants was utilized conducted at the research site. The protocol for all participants of the study was as follows:

- A three-day course on the requirements of C&A was conducted.

- Participants were divided into teams by the instructor and given a project assignment.

- Upon completion of the assignment, participants took approximately 30 minutes to complete the TEP and demographic questionnaires.

- Cycle time was self-reported by team members.

- The instructor evaluated the assignment deliverable for completeness and provided a quality score for each team.

Chapter 5

Analysis of Data

This chapter describes the data and the analysis conducted to examine the relationship between the independent and dependent variables to determine if the data provided sufficient support to warrant further testing of the proposed hypotheses.

First, an analysis of the sample is presented. Due to the convenience sampling employed in this study and the resulting small samples obtained, the two samples of course participants were first evaluated to determine: (1) if they were representative of the same population, and (2) whether they could be combined in order to yield a sample size that could support statistical analysis.

5.1 Analysis of the Samples

As was discussed earlier, convenience sampling of the participants in the two sections of the course had the potential of yielding two small, non-representative samples. As a result, the researcher utilized non-parametric procedures (the Mann-Whitney U test and the Median test) to evaluate the two convenience samples to determine if they were representative of the same population.

To perform the Mann-Whitney U test, the raw scores for each of the dimensions of team effectiveness from the TEP surveys of the participants were rank ordered and analyzed (see Appendix F).

Group A was characteristically lower in all rankings for all dimensions; however, these differences were not statistically significant, suggesting that the two groups were representative of the same population.

The Median test, another non-parametric procedure that tests for the differences between samples, was used to validate the results of the Mann-Whitney U test. The Median test used the raw score, for each of the dimensions as the basis of analysis. The results of the Median test confirmed that the two convenience samples were representative of the same population, showing no significant differences between the two. These results are presented in Appendix F.

The results of these two tests confirmed the comparability of the two convenience samples. Since this analysis did not show any significant differences between the groups, the two samples were combined into a single sample, in order to test the hypotheses.

5.2 Analysis of Relationships

5.2.1 Descriptive Analysis of Team Effectiveness and Team Performance

Table 10 summarizes both team effectiveness and performance data for each of the teams, and lists the composite scores for each group, using data from the TEP survey and the group project. Cycle time is presented in hours. Both the TEP scores and the scores for each dimension of the TEP were calculated by utilizing the scoring methodology prescribed by the TEP. Individual dimension scores could range from 10 to 50. The TEP scores could range from 50 to 250. The numerical quality score assigned by the instructor ranged from 0 to 100.

Initial evaluation of differences between the two groups suggested relationships

among the variables. As seen in Table 10, Group A, on average, scored lower than Group B

on the three key measures (TEP Score, Cycle Time, and Quality).

Table 10
Team Effectiveness and Team Performance Data

Group A	Mission, Vision, & Goals	Team Roles	Operating Processes	Intra-group Relationship	Inter-team Relationship	TEP Score	Cycle Time	Quality Score
Team 1	29.5	19.5	32	39.5	38	158.5	1.75	85
Team 2	44.5	31	43.5	41	42	202	2.0	80
Team 3	42	32	38.3	39.3	35.3	187	2.0	89
Team 4	36	28.5	33	37.3	32	166.7	1.3	100
Team 5	38	32.5	38	39.5	35	183	2.0	75
Team 6	38	30.5	42.5	38	26.5	175.5	2.0	75
Team 7	34.5	32.5	34	36.5	33.5	171	1.5	75
Team 8	42	33.3	39	39.3	35	188.6	.75	90
Average	**38.1**	**30**	**37.5**	**38.8**	**34.7**	**179.0**	**1.66**	**84**
Group B								
Team 1	38.6	33.6	38.3	37.3	39.3	187.3	2.25	95
Team 2	46.3	35	43	43.3	39.3	207	2.25	95
Team 3	39	35	40	40.6	39.3	194	3.0	75
Team 4	34.3	25.6	34.3	37	34.6	166	2.25	100
Team 5	42.3	37	38.6	42.6	38.6	199.3	2.50	85
Average	**40.1**	**33.2**	**38.8**	**40.2**	**38.2**	**190.7**	**2.45**	**90**

To explore the nature of these relationships, the TEP scores were plotted against the cycle times (see Figure 2) and the quality scores (see Figure 3) for each team.

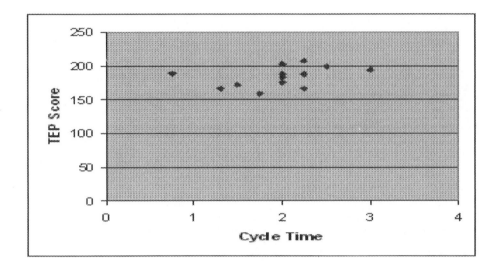

Figure 2. Team TEP Scores vs. Cycle Times

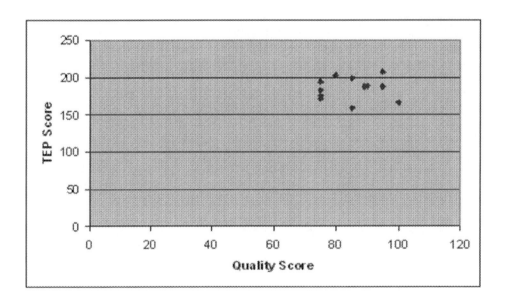

Figure 3. Team TEP Scores vs. Quality Scores

When composite scores for each group were evaluated in the same manner, the following observations were made:

- The higher the TEP Score the longer the cycle time (see Figure 4).

- The higher the TEP Score the higher the quality score (see Figure 5).

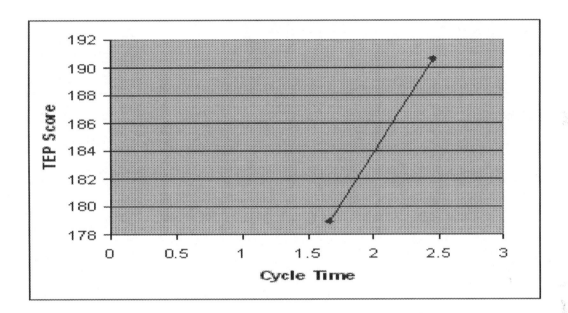

Figure 4. Group TEP Score vs. Cycle Time

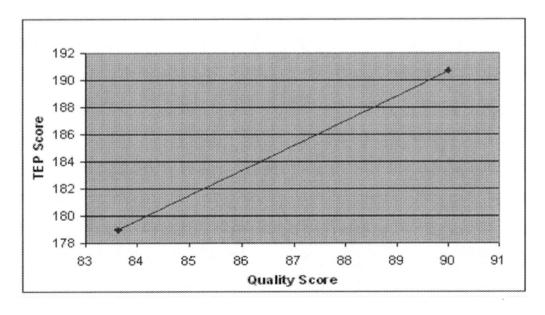

Figure 5. Group TEP Score vs. Quality Score

Team Profiles Based on TEP Score

Given this indication of relationships among the variables, a further examination of
the effectiveness of each team was conducted. Table 11 presents the frequency and
distribution of each group's effectiveness rating for each dimension of the TEP, as well as
the frequency distribution for the combined sample.

Table 11

Team Effectiveness As Perceived by Group A and Group B Participants

Dimension		Very Ineffective		Ineffective		Somewhat Effective		Effective		Very Effective	
		Freq.	%	Freq.	%	Freq.	%	Freq.	%	Freq.	%
Mission, Goal Setting, & Planning	Group A	1	5%	2	11%	7	37%	6	32%	3	16%
	Group B	0	0%	1	7%	4	27%	7	47%	3	20%
	Total	1	3%	3	9%	11	32%	13	38%	6	8%
Roles, Organization	Group A	6	32%	7	32%	6	32%	0	0%	0	0%
	Group B	3	20%	5	33%	3	20%	4	27%	0	0%
	Total	9	26%	12	35%	9	26%	4	12%	0	0%
Operating Processes	Group A	1	0%	3	16%	8	42%	7	37%	0	0%
	Group B	0	0%	1	7%	7	47%	7	47%	0	0%
	Total	1	3%	4	12%	15	44%	14	41%	0	0%
Intra-group Relationships	Group A	0	0%	0	0%	11	58%	8	42%	0	0%
	Group B	0	0%	0	0%	4	27%	11	73%	0	0%
	Total	0	0%	0	0%	15	44%	19	56%	0	0%
Inter-team Relations	Group A	3	16%	4	21%	9	47%	3	16%	0	0%
	Group B	0	0%	3	20%	5	33%	7	47%	0	0%
	Total	3	9%	7	21%	14	41%	10	29%	0	0%

Using the guidelines provided by the TEP instrument, the raw scores from these
group totals were interpreted using the Effectiveness Scale described in Chapter 4. Table 12
summarizes the group ratings using the Effectiveness Scale. As seen in Table 12, the
primary differences in the effectiveness ratings in the groups occurred with respect to the

team's understanding of its mission, vision, and goals as well as with respect to the intra-group relationships.

Table 12
Team Profiles Based on TEP Scores

Group	Mission, Vision, & Goals	Team Roles	Operating Processes	Intra-group Relationship	Inter-team Relations	TEP
Group A	Somewhat Ineffective	Ineffective	Somewhat Ineffective	Somewhat Ineffective	Somewhat Ineffective	Cohesive
Group B	Effective	Ineffective	Somewhat Ineffective	Effective	Somewhat Ineffective	Effective
Differences	*Yes			*Yes		*Yes

These two dimensions were the primary differentiators between the two groups in team effectiveness. Therefore, the data suggested the following relationships:

1. Teams with a clear understanding of the mission, vision, and goals of the task had higher levels of performance.

2. Teams with effective intra-group relationships had higher levels of performance.

To address the research questions and to determine if the proposed hypotheses warranted further investigation, relationships were evaluated using two measures of correlation. The Pearson r statistic was used to evaluate the raw scores (interval data) and the Spearman's *rho* statistic was used to evaluate the rank-ordered data (ordinal data). As was discussed earlier, the samples were combined for the purpose of this analysis. The results of these statistical analyses are presented in Appendix G.

5.2.2 Support for Hypothesis I & III

The data were evaluated with respect to the following hypotheses:

- H1: There will be a positive correlation between team effectiveness and the cycle time required to complete the System Security Plan (SSP).

- H3: There will be a positive correlation between an individual dimension of team effectiveness and the cycle time required to complete the System Security Plan (SSP).

Support for Hypothesis 1 was explored using both raw and rank-ordered data to identify whether a significant relationship existed between the reported cycle time and the perception of team effectiveness. Additionally, to determine support for Hypothesis III, each dimension of the TEP was evaluated for its relationship to cycle time. Although no statistically significant relationships were found to exist between cycle time and any of these variables, the raw data suggested that the findings were consistent with prior research as to the relationship between team effectiveness and cycle time (Janz, 1996; Ting, 1991).

5.2.3 Support for Hypothesis II & IV

The data were evaluated with respect to the following hypotheses:

- H2: There will be a positive correlation between team effectiveness and the quality of the SSP produced by the team.

- H4: There will be a positive correlation between an individual dimension of team effectiveness and the quality of the SSP produced by the team.

Support for Hypothesis II was explored using both raw and rank-ordered data to identify whether a significant relationship existed between the quality of the SSP and the perception of team effectiveness. To determine support for Hypothesis IV, each dimension of the TEP was evaluated for its relationship to quality. Although no statistically significant relationships were found to exist between quality and any of these variables, the raw data suggested that the findings were consistent with prior team effectiveness research (Ting, 1991).

Chapter 6

Research Results

This chapter examines the results and findings generated by the data analysis presented in Chapter 5.

6.1 Team Effectiveness and Team Performance

This study examined the relationship between team effectiveness and team performance. Team effectiveness was measured using the TEP score resulting from the instrument developed by Glaser and Glaser (1989). Team Performance was measured by the cycle time to produce an SSP in a simulated training environment and the quality of the SSP produced during the exercise.

Analysis of the raw data suggested the following relationships:

1. The higher the level of team effectiveness, the longer the cycle time.

2. The higher the level of team effectiveness, the higher the level of quality.

3. The greater the understanding of the team's mission, vision, and goals, the greater the level of performance of the team.

4. The stronger the intra-group relationships within a team, the greater the level of performance of the team.

The first two relationships identified were consistent with Ting's findings (1991). The relationships identified for the individual dimensions of team effectiveness were also supported in the literature as discussed in Chapter 2 (see Table 2). However, the examination of the stated hypotheses did not provide statistical support for any of the relationships identified.

Since this was exploratory research using a simulated team environment, it is possible that these results were affected by the convenience sampling and relatively small populations studied. In addition, it is not known whether the individuals attending these courses were representative of the population of certifiers performing in C&A teams, nor is it known if the composition of these teams (as assigned within the classroom context) were representative of typical C&A teams.

As noted in the discussion of rival hypotheses in Chapter 3, other factors may have affected the dynamics of the classroom environment, such as:

- Technical Competency: Although the case study did not require specific technical knowledge it is unknown if any teams had particular issues with the content of the project. Although C&A teams producing SSPs in the work place are typically small, the lack of skills and knowledge by one individual is often balanced by the expertise of other team members, which may not have been the case with the classroom team.

- Consequences: Although most attendees were sent to the training class due to C&A assignments, there were no negative or positive consequences related to performance during the course. It is unknown if all participants treated the project with the same level of concern that they would in the work environment.

- Time Scheduling: The course project was conducted on the last day of the three-day training course. Whether participants rushed through the project in order to take advantage of an early release is not known. Furthermore, it is possible that a participant's intention to leave early could have affected the dynamics of the team performance or effectiveness.

In summary, while statistical support for the hypotheses was not achieved, the analysis of the raw data provided insight into potential relationships among the variables. In particular, the data suggested that two dimensions of team effectiveness, the understanding of a team's mission, vision and goals, and the intra-group relationships -- have an influence on team performance.

Chapter 7

Implications of Results

Despite federal budgeting and mandated oversight of federal programs, information security programs still have not achieved their goal to establish effective security practices. FISMA evaluations of federal agencies have concentrated on the quantitative aspects of information security rather than the root causes of the slow progress observed for C&A processes. This study examined team effectiveness and its influence on team performance. Based upon the analysis conducted, this concluding chapter discusses how team effectiveness, and two of its dimensions in particular, should be addressed further to enhance information security C&A at federal agencies.

7.1 Contribution to Knowledge

This study served as an exploration of the relationships between team effectiveness and team performance in the information security environment. As a result of this exploratory research, Glaser's team effectiveness research was extended into this discipline.

The TEP was used to measure team effectiveness in the C&A environment. For future studies in the information security environment, this instrument can be used to assess the relative strengths and weaknesses of C&A teams. With further refinement, this assessment methodology can begin to answer questions about how to structure certification and accreditation teams in order to achieve acceptable quality SSPs, within reasonable cycle times.

This exploratory study specifically contributed the following:

- A framework for investigation of the relationship between team effectiveness and team performance in the C&A environment.

- The identification of two specific dimensions of team effectiveness (mission and goals; intra-group relationships) that may have a significant impact on the performance of C&A teams.

- The introduction of the TEP as a tool for the assessment of team effectiveness within the information security C&A environment, and its subsequent modification for a training environment.

This study also extended research in information security compliance by examining the relationship between certification team effectiveness and the quality of the SSP produced by the team. While previous research (Farah, 2004) explored the relationship between the status of FISMA compliance and the quality of the C&A process within the information security program, this study examined the dimensions of team effectiveness and their influence on the timeliness and quality of the output of that process (the SSP).

7.2 Implications for Future Research

Interdependent teams are critical to the successful implementation of security programs. In particular, the effectiveness of C&A teams is an important component in the context of protecting our nation's information infrastructure. This study was significant in bringing to light the dimensions of team effectiveness that warrant further investigation with respect to their relationship with team performance.

Additional study of the influence of the two dimensions of team effectiveness (mission, vision and goals, and intra-group relationships) is warranted due to the potential relationships with team performance that were found. The raw data evaluated and presented in Table 12 suggested that these two dimensions might be significant differentiators in the effectiveness of teams producing the SSP. The influence of these dimensions in the work environment should be researched further.

First, further investigation into the significance of the "Kick-off Meeting", also known as the system validation meeting, is recommended. In the C&A lifecycle process, this meeting is held to identify and document the mission, vision, and goals of a specific certification project and therefore may be a significant factor affecting the level of success of a C&A team. Secondly, the methods and means of communications within the C&A team need to be researched further, to investigate how teams can develop and optimize effective intra-group relations.

Although this study did not provide statistical support for the hypotheses presented, the raw data provided insight into possible relationships among the variables that may be verified through larger samples within training environments. However, team composition within training environments should be reviewed in order to ensure that they are representative of work teams normally assembled for C&A activities in the work environment. Furthermore, future researchers must carefully structure the study teams so that results can be aggregated to provide a statistically significant sample to produce meaningful results.

In addition, the potential influence of factors that are inherent a training environment suggests that more meaningful discovery would be accomplished through examination of existing C&A teams within the work environment. While other mitigating factors may arise in a work-based setting, a more realistic assessment of the influence of team effectiveness may result through such research.

Finally, further investigation of the characteristics of individual team members that may enhance team effectiveness is recommended. This includes demographic characteristics such as education, training and professional certifications, as well as personality characteristics that influence the effective communication and collaboration that are essential for effective intra-group relationships.

7.3 Implications for Practitioners

Creating effective teams is a significant factor in improving team performance in processes such as C&A. As suggested by the initial analysis of the data, two dimensions of team effectiveness (mission, vision and goals and intra-group relationships) emerged as possible differentiators in team performance. Managers of C&A teams need to assess these dimensions by asking the following questions:

- Do all team members clearly understand the mission, vision, and goals of the C&A project to which they are assigned?

- Are the intra-group relationships and communications open, direct, and supportive?

By evaluating these two components and implementing remedies for any deficiencies discovered, managers may see immediate improvement in the performance of their teams. The TEP instrument may prove to be a beneficial tool in helping managers in the assessment of a team's effectiveness. Managers and corporate trainers should be encouraged to investigate the applicability of the TEP to their environments.

Furthermore, C&A managers should reflect upon the five dimensions identified in the TEP framework and consider the following recommendations that may elicit improvement in the effectiveness of their C&A teams:

- Mission, vision and goals:

  The mission, vision, and goals of the federal agencies with respect to C&A need to be articulated and clearly communicated within the organization in order for the acceptable level of risk to be properly determined. Under these circumstances, when the C&A package is presented for approval, the authorizing authority will be better able to determine if the certified system is within the acceptable level of risk.

- Team Roles:

Farah's (2004) study indicated that lack of knowledge on the part of any team member affected the cycle of process improvement and resulted in poor outcomes of the C&A process. The C&A teams should have a clear and precise understanding of their roles regardingthe fundamentals of security certification and accreditation in order to produce a more accurate and complete SSP.

- Operating Processes:

Security certification is a comprehensive assessment of the management, operational, and technical security controls in an information system that is made in support of security; and accreditation determines the extent to which the controls are implemented correctly. NIST guidelines identify skills and knowledge of the security process as key attributes of C&A team members, particularly the Information System Security Officer (ISSO) (NIST, 2004). Effective training helps to create the team culture needed to support both the evolution of technology and the practices consistent with policies concerning acceptable levels of risk. Therefore, agencies must ensure that all team members have adequate training to support their assigned responsibilities.

- Intra-group Relationships:

Intra-group relationships are key to a successful security accreditation as part of a dynamic, ongoing risk management process. In order to develop effective intra-group relationships, agencies must inspire camaraderie within teams through social interaction.

- Inter-team Relations:

  Effective communication among geographically dispersed C&A teams is critical

  to achieve the level of knowledge sharing that is essential to appropriately support

  and certify the diverse systems within an agency. Agencies must recognize the

  interdependency among C&A teams and facilitate communications that enhance

   inter-team relationships.

7.4 Conclusions

In the C&A environment, where timely production of quality SSPs is critical to the

protection of the nation's infrastructure, the performance of C&A teams needs to be

dramatically improved. Team effectiveness has been shown to have considerable influence

on the performance of teams in other environments. This exploratory research provided

insight on the role of team effectiveness in the success of C&A teams in accomplishing

much needed performance improvement.

The data collected in this study suggested that a relationship existed between team

effectiveness and certification team performance, indicating that further research to explore

the proposed hypotheses is warranted. Furthermore, the data suggested that, in particular,

the role of mission, vision and goals and intra-group relationships are key to the

development of effective teams; therefore these dimensions should be addressed. Since the

C&A environment relies on the C&A team performance for successful information security

compliance, this researcher believes that it is critical for organizations involved in these

activities to recognize the important role team effectiveness plays in the successful

completion of these duties.

Increasing management awareness of the role of team effectiveness in information security, could lead to operational benefits such as decreased C&A backlogs, improved system tracking, and reduced information security program costs. Ultimately, creating a culture of effective teams can help to address the current problems associated with the unsatisfactory level of compliance with FISMA in federal agencies.

APPENDICES

Appendix A

Definitions of Terms

The source of these definitions is the National Security Telecommunications and Information Systems Security Committee (NSTISSI) 4009.

Accreditation: Formal declaration by a Designated Accrediting Authority (DAA) that an IT system is approved to operate in a particular security mode using a prescribed set of safeguards.

Assurance: Measure of confidence that the security features and architecture of an IT system accurately mediate and enforce the security policy.

Availability: The property of a resource being accessible and usable upon demand by an authorized user.

Audit: Independent review and examination of records and activities to assess the adequacy of system controls, to ensure compliance with established policies and operational procedures, and to recommend necessary changes in controls, policies, or procedures.

Certification: Comprehensive evaluation of the technical and non-technical security features of an IT system and other safeguards made in support of the accreditation process to establish the extent to which a particular design and implementation meets a set of specified security requirements.

Confidentiality: The property that information is not made available or disclosed to unauthorized individuals, entities, or processes.

Environment: The aggregate of external procedures, conditions, and objects that affect the development, operation, and maintenance of a system.

Information System: Any telecommunication or computer-related equipment or interconnected system or subsystems of equipment that is used in the acquisition, storage, manipulation, management, movement, control, display, switching, interchange, transmission, or reception of voice and/or data; includes software, firmware, and hardware.

Information System Security Officer (ISSO): The person responsible to the Designated Accrediting Authority (DAA) who ensures that an IT system is approved, operated, and maintained in accordance with the System Security Authorization Agreement (SSAA).

Information Technology (IT): The hardware, firmware, and software used as part of the information system to perform DOD information functions. This definition includes computers, telecommunications, automated information systems, and automatic data processing equipment. IT includes any assembly of computer hardware, software, and/or firmware configured to collect, create, communicate, compute, disseminate, process, store, and/or control data or information.

Integrity: The property that allows the preservation of known unaltered states between baseline certifications and allows information, access, and processing service to function according to specified expectations. It is composed of data integrity and system integrity.

Mission: The assigned duties to be performed by a resource.

Risk: A combination of the likelihood that a threat will occur, the likelihood that a threat occurrence will result in an adverse impact, and the severity of the resulting impact.

Risk Assessment: Process of analyzing threats to and vulnerabilities of an IT system, and the potential impact that the loss of information or capabilities of a system would have on a national security and using the analysis as a basis for identifying appropriate and cost-effective measures.

Risk Management: Process concerned with the identification, measurement, control, and minimization of security risks in IT systems.

Security: Measures and controls that ensure confidentiality, integrity, availability, and accountability of the information processed and stored by a computer.

Security Process: The series of activities that monitor, evaluate, test, certify, accredit, and maintain the system accreditation throughout the system life cycle.

Security Requirements: Types and levels of protection necessary for equipment, data, information, applications, and facilities to meet security policy.

Security Specification: Detailed description of the safeguards required to protect an IT system.

System: The set of interrelated components consisting of mission, environment, and architecture as a whole.

System Integrity: The attribute of a system when it performs its intended function in an unimpaired manner, free from deliberate or inadvertent unauthorized manipulation of the system.

Threat: Capabilities, intentions, and attack methods of adversaries to exploit, or any circumstance or event with the potential to cause harm to, information or an information system.

User: The individual or organization that operates or uses the resources of an information system.

Validation: Determination of the correct implementation in the completed IT system with the security requirements and approach agreed upon by the users, acquisition authority, and the Designated Accrediting Authority (DAA).

Verification: The process of determining the compliance of the evolving IT system specification, design, or code with the security requirements and approach agreed on by the users, acquisition authority, and the Designated Accrediting Authority (DAA).

Appendix B

List of Symbols and Acronyms

ACRONYMS	DEFINITIONS
C&A	Certification and Accreditation
CIA	Central Intelligence Agency
CIA	Confidentiality, Integrity, and Availability
DAA	Designated Accrediting Authority
DBMS	Database Management System
DCID	Director of Central Intelligence Directive
DII	Defense Information Infrastructure
DoD	Department of Defense
FISMA	Federal Information Security Management Act
GAO	General Accounting Office
IG	Inspector General
IRM	Information Resource Management
IS	Information System
ISSO	Information System Security Officer
IT	Information Technology
LOC	Level of Concern
NIST	National Institute of Standards and Technology
NSTI	National Security Training Institute
NSTISSI	National Security Telecommunications and Information Systems Security
OMB	Office of Management and Budget
PL	Protection Level
SCI	Sensitive Compartmented Information
SSP	System Security Plan
ST&E	Security Test and Evaluation
TEP	Team Effectiveness Profile
COMSEC	Communications Security
DIRNSA	Director, National Security Agency
EMSEC	Emissions Security
SSAA	System Security Authorization Agreement

Appendix C

Instruments

Sample DCID 6/3 Team Training Course

Part A: Matrix of Minimum Security Specification

Explanation: This matrix is used to identify a <u>minimum</u> set of safeguards that should be implemented to protect classified and sensitive application systems and general support systems. Justification for non-implementation of these safeguards should be based on the results of a formal risk analysis, risk assessment, and cost-benefit analysis.

Directions: Scan the X s and Os beneath each security level designation. An X means that the security safeguard listed to the left is a requirement. An O means that the security safeguard is optional.

	CONTROLS	SECURITY LEVEL			
		Classified (Level 1)	High Sensitivity (Level 2)	Moderate Sensitivity (Level 2)	Low Sensitivity (Level 2)
	MANAGEMENT CONROLS				
1.	Establish a detailed risk management program	X	X	X	O
2.	Ensure that all personnel positions have been assigned security level designations	X	X	X	X
3.	Conduct periodic security level designation reviews	X	X	X	O
4.	Ensure that all personnel, including contractors, have received appropriate clearances.	X	X	X	O
5.	Maintain a list of all "classified," "Special-Sensitive," and "Critical-Sensitive" clearances granted.	X	X	O	O
6.	Conduct formal risk analyses (Host computer/network).	X	X	X	O
7.	Conduct application risk assessment.	X	X	X	X
8.	Prepare and document application rules of behavior	X	X	X	X
9.	Maintain accurate inventory of all hardware and software.	X	X	X	X
SECURITY AWARENESS AND TRAINING					

		SECURITY LEVEL			
	CONTROLS	Classified (Level 1)	High Sensitivity (Level 2)	Moderate Sensitivity (Level 2)	Low Sensitivity (Level 2)
1.	Establish an employee security awareness and training program.	X	X	X	X
2.	Provide specialized security training	X	X	O	O
DEVELOPMENT/IMPLEMENTATION CONTROLS					
1.	Prepare security specifications.	X	X	X	O
2.	Conduct application design review and system testing.	X	X	X	X
3.	Conduct a security review and prepare a certification report	X	X	X	X
OPERATIONAL CONTROLS					
1.	Ensure that a complete and current set of documentation exists for all operating systems.	X	X	X	X
2.	Establish controls over the handling of sensitive data, including labeling materials and controlling the availability and flow of data.	X	X	X	O
3.	Require that all sensitive material be stored in a secure location when not in use.	X	X	X	O
4.	Dispose of unneeded sensitive hard copy documents and erase sensitive data from storage media in a manner that will prevent unauthorized use.	X	X	X	O

	CONTROLS	SECURITY LEVEL			
		Classified (Level 1)	High Sensitivity (Level 2)	Moderate Sensitivity (Level 2)	Low Sensitivity (Level 2)
5.	Prepare and maintain lists of persons authorized to access facilities and automated information systems processing sensitive data.	X	X	X	O
6.	Establish procedures for controlling access to facilities and automated information systems processing sensitive data.	X	X	X	X
7.	Furnish locks and other protective measures on doors and windows to prevent unauthorized access to computer and support areas.	X	X	X	X
8.	Install emergency (panic) hardware on "emergency exit only" doors. Ensure that emergency exits are appropriately marked.	X	X	X	X
9.	Specify fire-rated walls, ceilings, and doors for construction of new computer facilities or modification of existing facilities.	X	X	O	O
10.	Install smoke/fire detection systems with alarms in the computer facility. When feasible, connect all alarms to a control alarm panel within the facility and to a manned guard station or fire station.	X	X	O	O
11.	Install fire suppression equipment in the computer facility that may include area sprinkler systems with protected control valves, and/or fire extinguishers.	X	X	X	O

	CONTROLS	SECURITY LEVEL			
		Classified (Level 1)	High Sensitivity (Level 2)	Moderate Sensitivity (Level 2)	Low Sensitivity (Level 2)
12.	Provide emergency power shut down controls to shut down AIS equipment and air conditioning systems in the even of fire or other emergencies. Include protective covers for emergency controls to prevent accidental activation.	X	X	X	O
13.	Provide waterproof covers to protect computers and other electronic equipment from water damage.	X	X	O	O
14.	Establish a fire emergency preparedness plan to include training of fire emergency response teams, development and testing of an evacuation plan, and on site orientation visits for the local fire department.	X	X	X	O
15.	Establish contingency plan and information back-up plan.	X	X	X	X
16.	Establish emergency power program	X	X	O	O
17.	Configuration management and application software maintenance	X	X	X	X
18.	SDLC documentation	X	X	X	O
TECHNICAL CONTROLS					
1.	Require use of current passwords and log on codes to protect sensitive automated information systems data from unauthorized access.	X	X	X	O

		SECURITY LEVEL			
	CONTROLS	Classified (Level 1)	High Sensitivity (Level 2)	Moderate Sensitivity (Level 2)	Low Sensitivity (Level 2)
2.	Establish procedures to register and protect secrecy of passwords and log on codes, including the use of a non-print, feature.	X	X	X	O
3.	Limit the number of unsuccessful attempts to access an automated information system or a database.	X	X	X	O
4.	Develop means whereby the user's authorization can be determined. (This may include answer back capability.)	X	X	X	O
5.	Establish an automated audit trail capability to record user activity.	X	X	X	O
6.	Implement methods, which may include the establishment of encryption, to secure data being transferred between two points	X	X	O	O
7.	Ensure that the operating system contains controls to prevent unauthorized access to the executive or control software system.	X	X	X	O
8.	Ensure that the operating system contains controls that separate user and master modes of operations.	X	X	X	O
9.	Record occurrences of non-routine user/operator activity (such as unauthorized access attempts and operator overrides) and report to the organizational ISSO.	X	X	O	O

		SECURITY LEVEL			
	CONTROLS	Classified	High Sensitivity	Moderate Sensitivity	Low Sensitivity
		(Level 1)	(Level 2)	(Level 2)	(Level 2)
10.	Ensure that the operating system provides methods to protect operational status and subsequent restart integrity during and after shutdown.	X	X	O	O
11.	Install software feature(s) that will automatically lock out the terminal if it is not used for a predetermined period of lapsed inactive time, for a specified time after normal closing time, or if a password is not entered correctly after a specified number of times.	X	X	X	O
12.	Ensure that the operating system contains controls to secure the transfer of data between all configuration devices.	X	O	O	O
13.	Secure communication lines	X	O	O	O
14.	Ensure that VIRUS protection procedures are in place and users are trained in virus prevention	X	X	X	X
15.	Implement required access control procedures for public use of the system.	X	X	X	X
16.	Review security and effectiveness of FIREWALLS	X	X	X	X
17.	Prepare written authorization for interconnection with other systems and sharing of sensitive information	X	X	X	X

Part B: Security Standards

This table is extracted from Federal documents to illustrate the major statutory and regulatory references for the basic computer security functions.

Basic Security Functions	Computer Security Act 1987	OMB Circ. A-130	A-123 A-127	FPM	FIRMR	PA/FOIA	NIST Pubs
Policy Implement and maintain security program; assign responsibilities		X			X	X	
Security Plans Identify sensitive system; implement security plans	X				X		800-18
Applications Security Certify applications; re-certify every 3 years. Develop and maintain contingency plans.		X X	X		X X		73, 102 87

Basic Security Functions	Computer Security Act 1987	OMB Circ. A-130	A-123 A-127	FPM	FIRMR	PA/FOIA	NIST Pubs
Installation Security Conduct risk analysis every 3 years. Prepare acquisition specifications. Maintain disaster recover plans.		X X X	X		X X		31,65 87
Personnel Security Designate sensitive positions and screen incumbents		X		X	X		
Security Awareness and Training Train Federal and contractor personnel.	X	X					800-16
Reporting Report security weaknesses in A-123 Report to President		X	X				

Note. The Computer Security Act of 1987 is implemented through OMB Bulletins and other regulatory material. NIST Special Publication 800-18 outlines the contents of security plans.

Part C: Certification Process Outline

The process for certifying systems or applications should be properly planned, initiated, and managed. This section highlights the steps for this process.

Assign a Project Leader

A successful certification process starts with the assignment of a certification project leader. The project leader is normally the organization's information systems security officer (ISSO). For new and significantly modified systems or applications, the project leader performs certification work in conjunction with the system application development team.

Initiate a Project Charter

The security charter includes the scope of work to be performed by the participants, the resources needed, the work plan or schedule, and the sponsor. The project charter is the basis for obtaining formal authorization to proceed, acquiring resources, orienting project participants, and reaching a consensus within the organization of the project scope and context. This document may be part of the overall application development charter.

The project leader should circulate the charter to all organizational components that will be involved in the certification process.

Documentation Review

The project team reviews existing security documents for the target system or application and those host systems to which the system or application connects to, to help determine safeguards that are in place, planned, or not applicable. These documents include:

1) Security Plan: A computer security plan summarizes security and privacy requirements of the system or application under consideration and describes the controls in place or planned for meeting those requirements. The plan also delineates responsibilities and expected behavior of all individuals who access the system. The OMB recommended format includes four basic sections: System Identification, Management Controls, Operational Controls, and Technical Controls. Security Plans and their content will be discussed in more detail in the accreditation section.

2) Risk Assessment: The analysis of threats, vulnerabilities, assets, and safeguards, as they affect systems or applications determines their risk. If the system or application has not had a risk assessment completed, this fact should be cited.

3) System Test and Evaluation (ST&E): The ST&E is a critical element of the certification process. This element tests the effectiveness of safeguards that have been implemented to protect the system or application. If a ST&E has been done previously, this document should be reviewed and updated where necessary.

4) Contingency/Disaster Recovery Plan: An existing plan may be updated to meet the requirement. If none exits, it should be documented in the security plan as a "planned" safeguard and included in the Certification/Accreditation Statement as a planned action.

5) Audits, Reviews, and Re-Certifications: Systems and applications must be re-certified at least every three years. Review of this documentation may identify limitations on the system or application that may not be general knowledge or detected previously.

6) Management Reviews: These include departmental and OA Information Resource Management (IRM) reviews and related activities.

7) Inspector General (IG) Audit Reviews: The IG conducts several audits and reviews each year, including computer security audits. Review of this documentation may identify limitations on the system or application that may not be general knowledge or detected previously.

8) Systems Life-Cycle Technical Documents: These are prepared to support the development, operation, and maintenance of the system that should be reviewed to support the certification review. These include among others:

      a. Functional Requirements Analysis

      b. Design Specifications

      c. Hardware and Software Configuration

      d. Testing and Acceptance Documentation

      e. Systems Manual and User Manual

Design Reviews and System Tests and Evaluation

Design reviews and system tests are methods of determining the cost as well as the technical efficiency of safeguards for a system or application. These reviews should be conducted prior to filing for a final "Authority to Operate". This is to assure that the system or application has made an effort to mitigate their "unacceptable risk" and that the safeguards implemented are mission enhancing and effective.

1) DESIGN REVIEWS

The purpose of the design review is to ensure that all safeguards have been incorporated into the application system during the design phase.

The purpose of the design phase is to determine how best to satisfy requirements. The primary security goal is to ensure that system requirements are adequately incorporated into the design specifications, including controls that ensure auditability.[1] the design team determines how the system will work, addressing the components, subsystems, and modules. An application system is usually technology environment component that is composed of multiple systems, various hardware, software, and networking elements. Application security must therefore be implemented from a comprehensive, system-wide viewpoint. Components of a major application system may include multiple applications, a database management system (DBMS), a host computer, and a network.

Security requirements may be designed into the system in various ways. For example, authentication control, or passwords, may depend entirely on the operating system controls or a combination of DBMS, computer operating system, and the network operating system controls. When the desired hardware and software combinations do not provide sufficient security, special products may be added to the system, such as RACF or Top Secret for mainframes, Watchdog Director or Net-DAC for networks, or PC-DAC for PC's.

To facilitate a design review, as required by OMB Circular A-130, the documentation should show where and how the security specifications are implemented. The design review is the last reasonable opportunity to identify weak points in the security plan. Omissions or inadequacies in the security feature if the design that is not identified in the design review may require costly software modifications.

2) SYSTEM TESTS

System testing is the means by which the effectiveness of implemented safeguards can be tested, validated, and reported. These test results will also allow managers the ability determines if the return on investment for a specific safeguard is economically feasible.

Testing could include both static and dynamic procedures, such as:

a) Static evaluation techniques, which include:

- Conduct of tests for each security safeguard
- Conduct of penetration studies to find security flaws
- Review of code compliance with design specifications

b) Dynamic testing means the operation of the application system with test data and the comparison of the actual results with expected or known results.

c) Specifications, Tests, and Results

Appendix D

Demographic Questionnaire

Thank you for participating in this study. The purpose of this study is to examine the impact of team effectiveness on team performance in the certification and accreditation process.

This survey will measure the team effectiveness profile of your team for this course project. Your participation in this survey should take approximately 15 to 30 minutes.

All responses will be kept strictly confidential. You will not be obligated to provide any personally identifying information. The information collected in this survey will only be published in aggregate form. If you have any questions, ask the monitor for assistance. Your participation in this survey is sincerely appreciated.

Demographic Information

Please provide the appropriate answers regarding you and your team.

Your initials: _____
Your Team Number: _____
Number of Team Members:_____
Time to complete project:_ _____

Please check the appropriate answers for these ten questions.

1. Please indicate your gender:

        Female   Male

2. Please indicate your age range: (*Check only one.*)

        Under 25   25-35   36-45   46-54   55 or older

3. Please indicate the highest level of education you have completed: (*Check only one.*)

        HS/GED   Bachelor's   Master's   PhD   Other _____

4. Please indicate the professional certifications you hold: (*Check all that apply.*)
CISSP   CNA   CISM   CISA   CFE   CCNE   MCSE
Other(s) _____

5. Please check the number of years of experience you have in writing or creating system security plans using any federal standard methodology: (*Check only one.*)

    None   Less than 1 year   1 year   2 years   3 years   5 or more years

6. Please indicate what motivated you to attend this training: (*Check all that apply.*)

        Required by your customer
        Required by your employer
        Desire career advancement
        Desire personal development
        Other _____

7. If all members of a work group possess the following security characteristics:

- same level of SCI clearances,
- same level of access control, and
- same "need to know",

What Level of Protection (PL) would be required for this work group's information system? (*Check only one.*)

        PL1   PL2   PL3   PL4   PL5   None of the above
        Unsure

8. If all members of a working group possess the following security characteristics:

- same level of SCI clearance,
- same level of access control, but
- do not have the same "need to know",

What level of Protection (PL) would be required for this work group's information system? (*Check only one.*)

PL1	PL2	PL3	PL4
PL5	None of the above		Unsure

9. Please indicate your career field: (*Check all that apply.*)

Auditing   Information Security   Information Technology
Other _____

10. Please indicate the level of security in your work environment: (*Check only one.*)

Classified Only   Classified & Unclassified   Unclassified Only

---

Thank you for taking the time to respond to this survey!

Appendix E

Team Effectiveness Profile Description
4th Edition

Help teams learn how to surface, diagnose, and work through the issues that impede effective teamwork. For more than 15 years, the *Team Effectiveness Profile* (TEP) has helped teams eliminate or reduce blockages in the 5 vital areas of team activity: Mission, Vision, and Goals; Team Roles; Operating Processes; Interpersonal Relationships; Inter-team Relationships.

Learning Outcomes

- Identify issues that block effectiveness

- Reduce or eliminate problems that can drain a group's energy

- Maximize the group's productive efforts

Theory

The *Team Effectiveness Profile* focuses on the 5 Categories of Team Effectiveness. The first 4 of these categories are based on those presented by Richard Beckhard in Organization Development: Strategies and Models (1969). Inter-team relationship theory is the basis for the fifth category.

5 Categories of Team Effectiveness

- Mission, Vision and Goals

- Team Roles

- Operating Processes

- Interpersonal Relationships

- Inter-team Relationships

How It Works

The TEP has been designed to function as a self-administered learning instrument. The TEP yields an overall Team Effectiveness Score as well as separate scores for each of the 5 areas indicating the general health of the group and blockages that hinder team effectiveness.

Uses for the TEP

Appropriate for any type of team and all levels of team members and leaders, the TEP can be used as a stand-alone instrument or as a component in a larger team-building program. The TEP can be used to:

- Measure pre-team building conditions

- Orient new teams to potential problems

- Unblock struggling teams

- Determine post- team-building results

We recommend administering the TEP periodically, as issues will change over a period a time. Sited: http://www.hrdq.com/products/tep.htm

Team Effectiveness Profile Sample Items

The *Team Effectiveness Profile* is designed to enable teams to assess the effectiveness of its work. Using the response key, participants respond to 50 statements about how their team generally operates. Below are 5 sample statements taken from the participant booklet:

To enable you to assess the effectiveness of your project team please evaluate your group against each of the following statements using the descriptions below.

Response Key

5 = Always - Team always did this

4 = Usually - Team usually did this

3 = Sometimes - Team sometimes did this

2 = Usually Not - Team usually did not do this

1 = Never - Team never did this

Sample Items

Sample item relating to "Group Mission, Planning, and Goal Setting":

We periodically review our progress toward our goals.

Sample item relating to "Group Roles":

When individual roles change, an intentional effort is made to clarify these changes for everyone in the work group.

Sample item relating to "Group Operating Processes":

We are able to resolve our conflicts and disagreements collaboratively within our work group.

Sample item relating to "Group Interpersonal Relationships":

Group members help each other find professional satisfaction from the group's work.

Sample item relating to "Inter-team Relations":

Our group often has problems coordinating its efforts with other work groups.

Appendix F

Sample Analysis

Mann-Whitney U Test – Between Group Comparisons

Dimension	Group A Mean Rank	Group B Mean Rank	Mann-Whitney U	Wileoxon W	Z	2-tailed Significance (p=.025)
Mission	6.25	8.20	14.00	50.00	-.881	.378
Roles	5.38	9.60	7.00	43.00	-1.908	.056
Processes	6.31	8.10	14.50	50.50	-.806	.420
Intra-group	6.31	8.10	14.50	50.50	-.808	.419
Inter-team	5.63	9.20	9.00	45.00	-1.621	.105
TEP	5.88	8.80	11.00	47.00	-1.317	.188

Median Test – Between Group Comparisons

Dimension	Mean	Standard Deviation	Median	Exact Significance
Mission	38.854	4.617	38.70	.592
Roles	31.231	4.594	32.50	.032
Processes	38.050	3.784	38.30	.592
Intra-group	39.338	2.147	39.30	.592
Inter-team	36.05	4.048	35.30	.103
TEP	183.538	15.117	18.70	.103

Appendix G

Correlation Analysis

Correlation Analysis for Cycle Time

Dimension	Pearson R	Significance (2 tailed, p=.025)	Spearman's *rho*	Significance (2 tailed, p=.025)
Mission	.097	.587	.204	.248
Team Role	.176	.320	.231	.188
Process	.222	.207	.256	.144
Intra Team	.244	.163	.285	.102
Inter Team	.278	.112	.333	.054
TEP	.245	.163	.322	.063

Correlation Analysis for Quality

Dimension	Pearson R	Significance (2 tailed, p=.025)	Spearman's *rho*	Significance (2 tailed, p=.025)
Mission	.005	.977	-.026	.886
Team Role	-.152	.392	-.169	.338
Process	-.214	.225	-.245	.162
Intra Team	-.114	.521	-.146	.411
Inter Team	.012	.948	.004	.983
TEP	-.110	.535	-.115	.516

Reference List

Almond, G., & Verba, S. (1963). *The civic culture: Political attitudes and democracy in five nations.* Princeton, NJ: Princeton University Press.

Anderson, C., & Franks, N. R. (2001). Teams in animal societies. *Behavioral Ecology, 12,* 534–540.

Anderson, C., Franks, R. N., & McShea, D. W. (2001). The complexity and hierarchical structure of tasks in insect societies. *Animal Behavior, 62,* 643–651.

Blackburn, J. D., Scudder, G. D., & Van Wassenhove, L. N. (1996). Improving speed and productivity in software development: A global survey of software developers. *IEEE Transactions on Software Engineering, 22*(12), 875-885.

Buchholz, S., & Roth, T. (1987). *Creating the high performance team.* New York: John Wiley & Sons.

Central Intelligence Agency. (2000). *Director of Central Intelligence Directive 6/3: Protecting sensitive compartmented information within information systems.* Washington, DC: Director of Central Intelligence.

Cramton, C. D., & Webber, S. S. (2005). Relationships among geographic dispersion, team processes, and effectiveness in software development work teams. *Journal of Business Research, 58,* 758-765.

Dyer, W. G. (1987). *Team building.* Menlo Park, CA: Addison-Wesley Publishing Company.

Edmondson, A. C., Roberto, M. A., & Watkins, M. D. (2003). A dynamic model of top management team effectiveness: Managing unstructured task streams. *The Leadership Quarterly, 14,* 297-325.

Edwards, H. K., & Sridhar, V. (2003). Analysis of the effectiveness of global virtual teams in software engineering projects. *Symposium conducted at the meeting of the 36th Hawaii International Conference on Systems Sciences (HICSS'03),* Big Island, HI.

Farah, J. (2004). A study of the federal management community's awareness, attitudes, and understanding of information security requirement: Focus on FISMA best practices. *Dissertation Abstracts International, 65*(11), 5828. (UMI No. 3154015)

Fernandez, M. (2003). *The thinking together approach: An interpersonal model for cognition in the collaborative construction of web pages in history.* Paper presented at the International Conference on Computer Support for Collaborative Learning, 107-110.

Ferraiolo, K. M., Williams, J. R., & Landoll, D. J. (1994). *A capability maturity model for security engineering.* Paper presented at the Sixth Annual Canadian Computer Security Symposium. Ottawa, Canada.

Francis, D. & Young, D. (1979). *Improving work groups: A practical manual for team building.* San Diego, CA. University Associates, Inc.

Glaser, R. (1989). *Team effectiveness profile, trainer's guide.* King of Prussia, PA: Organization Design and Development Inc.

Glaser, R., & Glaser, C. (1989). *Team effectiveness profile.* King of Prussia, PA: Organization Design and Development Inc.

Grütter, A. W., Field, J. M., & Faull, N. H .B. (2002). Work team performance over time: Three case studies of South African manufacturers. *Journal of Operations Management, 20*, 641-657.

Harrison, D. A., Mohammed, S., McGrath, J. E., Florey, A. T., & Vanderstoep, S. W. (2003). Time matters in team performance: Effects of member familiarity, entrainment, and task discontinuity on speed and quality. *Personnel Psychology, 56*, 633-669.

Holton, J. A. (2001). Building trust and collaboration in a virtual team. *Team Performance Management, 7*(3/4), 36–47.

Hult, G. T. M., Frolick, M. N., & Nichols, E. L. (1995). Organizational learning and cycle time issues in the procurement process. *Cycle Time Research, 1*(1), 25-39.

Janz, B. D. (1996). Cooperative learning and cycle time reduction. *Cycle Time Research, 2*(1), 29-40.

Linderman, K., Schroeder, R. G., Choo, A. S. (in press). Six Sigma: The role of goals in improvement teams. *Journal of Operations Management.*

Maddux, R. (1989). *Team building*. London: Kogan Page Ltd., 1989.

Merriam-Webster's Online Dictionary, 10th ed. (2003). Retrieved October 6, 2006, from
http://www.m-w.com/

Nolan, V. (1989). *The innovator's handbook*. London: Sphere Books LTD.

Offermann, L. R., & Spiros, R. K. (in press). The science and practice of team
development: Improving the link. *Academy of Management Journal*.

Office of Management and Budget. (2002). *FY 2001 Report to Congress on Federal
Government Information Security Reform*. Washington, DC: Executive Office of
the President.

Office of Management and Budget. (2006). *FY 2005 Report to Congress on
Implementation of the Federal Information Security Management Act of 2002*.
Washington, DC: Executive Office of the President.

Office of Management and Budget. (2003). *Memorandum M-03-19: Reporting
instructions for the Federal Information Security Management Act and updated
guidance on quarterly IT security reporting*. Washington, DC: Executive Office
of the President.

Olsen, F. (2005, March 14). Feds brings home a D+: Security is still a tough assignment.
Federal Computer Week, Article 88268. Retrieved from:
[http://www.fcw.com/article88268]

Ramadorai, A., & Harris, J. (2003). Maximizing your engineering productivity.
Industrial Management, 45 (4).

Rangarajan, D., Chonko, L. B., Jones, E., & Roberts, J. A. (2004). Organizational
variables, sales force perceptions of readiness for change, learning, and
performance among boundary-spanning teams: A conceptual framework and
propositions for research. *Industrial Marketing Management, 33*, 289-305.

Ross, R., Swanson, M., Stoneburner, G., Katzke, S., & Johnson, A. (2004). *Guide for the
security certification and accreditation of Federal Information Systems*. (NIST
Special Publication 800-37). Washington, DC: US Department of Commerce.

Sashkin, M. & Burke, W. W. (1987). Organization development in the 1980s. *Journal of
Management, 13*, 393-417.

Syamil, A., Doll, W. J., & Apigian, C. H. (2004). Process performance in product
development: measures and impacts. *European Journal of Innovation
Management, 7*(3), 205-217.

Ting, H. M. (1991). The relationship between team effectiveness and simulated job performance in a high-technology semiconductor company. *Dissertation Abstracts International, 52* (05), 1818. (UMI No. 9128435)

Trent, R. J. (2004, March-April). Becoming an effective teaming organization. *Business Horizons 47*(2), 33-40.

Varney, G. H. (1989). *Building productive teams.* Oxford, England: Jossey-Bass Limited.

Werner, J. M. & Lester, S. W. (2001). Applying a team effectiveness framework to the performance of student case teams. *Human Resource Development Quarterly, 12*(4). 385-402.

Wetherbe, J. C. (1995). Principles of cycle time reduction: You can have your cake and eat it too. *Cycle Time Research, 1* (1).

Winder, Richard. E. & Judd, Daniel. K. (1996). *Organizational orienteering: Linking Deming, Covey, and Senge in an integrated five dimension quality model.* Paper presented at the 1996 Seventh National American Society for Quality Conference on quality management transactions. Retrieved from: http://www.ldri.com/articles/96orgorient.html

Biography

Barbara E. Banks-Burton has over 25 years of experience in Information Systems including over 12 years in Information Security. Currently, she serves as the Information Systems Security Manager for Lockheed Martin Corporation where she is responsible for certifying and accrediting systems and ensuring FISMA compliance for over 40 sites.

Previously, she held information technology positions of increasing responsibility for organizations including Computer Sciences Corporation and DynCorp.

Barbara earned a BS in Computer Information Systems from Virginia State University, a Master's in Business and Public Administration (MBP) from Howard University, and an MS in Information Security Technology from Eastern Michigan University.

In addition, Barbara holds a variety of professional certifications including: Certified Information Security Manager (CISM); Certified Business Manager (CBM); Certified Homeland Security (CHS III); NSA Information Assessment Methodology (IAM); Certified Computer Examiner (CCE); and UNIX Certified Systems Professional. In 2005, she became a Computer Forensics Examiner.

Printed in the United States
by Baker & Taylor Publisher Services